Mel Bay Presents
Young Beginner's First Repertoire For Classic Guitar

By Sonia Michelson

A recording of the music in this book is now available. The publisher strongly recommends the use of this recording along with the text to ensure accuracy of interpretation and ease in learning.

© 1996 BY MEL BAY PUBLICATIONS, INC., PACIFIC, MO 63069.
ALL RIGHTS RESERVED. INTERNATIONAL COPYRIGHT SECURED. B.M.I. MADE AND PRINTED IN U.S.A.

Visit us on the Web at http://www.melbay.com — E-mail us at email@melbay.com

Preface

The goal of this book of graded pieces is to present interesting compositions of intrinsic musical and technical value for young students. An effort has been made to present a wide variety of music in many styles and from different periods.

The music is carefully arranged in a graded sequence according to difficulty. Young students will enjoy making musical progress in playing pieces from Grade I through approximately Grade 2.

I have spent many years looking for attractive beginning pieces of high musical quality for my students. I am now happy to be able to share this music with other teachers and their young students.

Sonia Michelson

---

*Strive to play
easy pieces well
and beautifully;*

*it is better than
to render harder
pieces only
indifferently well.*

Robert Schumann

Contents

GRADE 1

Echos	Stepán Rak	5
Simple Arpeggios	Reginald Smith Brindle	6
Aeolian Mode	Reginald Smith Brindle	7
Moon Magic	Sonia Michelson	8
No. 1 from Three Arpeggio Studies	Reginald Smith Brindle	10
Starobylá	Stepán Rak	11
Country Dance	Reginald Smith Brindle	12
Misty Dawn	Sonia Michelson	13
Allegretto op. 44 no. 2	Fernando Sor	14
Welcome	Gérard Montreuil	15
Allegretto	Ferdinand Carulli	16
Waltz op. 121 no. 1	Ferdinand Carulli	17
Free With The Wind	Sonia Michelson	18
Danse Russe	Traditional	19
Andante	Anonymous	20
Here Comes The Band	Sonia Michelson	21

GRADE 2

Study in C	Fernando Sor	22
Sometimes I Hear A Song	Sonia Michelson	23
Andante op. 31 no. 1	Fernando Sor	24
Andante op. 35 no. 1	Fernando Sor	25

Allegretto	Fernando Sor	26
English Dance	Ferdinand Carulli	27
Ecossaise op. 33 no. 10	Mauro Giuliani	28
Andantino	Matteo Carcassi	29
Allegro op. 50 no. 13	Mauro Giuliani	30
Etude	Matteo Carcassi	31
Prelude op. 114	Ferdinand Carulli	32
Menuett	J. Krieger	33
Estudio in Am	D. Aguado	34
Andante	Matteo Carcassi	35
Gigue	J. Logy	36
Waltz	Ferdinand Carulli	37
Contre Danse	Ferdinand Carulli	38
Vals	Bartolome Calatayud	39
Minuet in G	J.S. Bach	40
Austrian Dance	Anonymous	41
Prelude in D	Sonia Michelson	42
German Dance	Anonymous	43
Moonlight	Stepán Rak	44
English Dance	Anonymous	45
Spanish Romance	Anonymous	46
Canario	Carlo Calvi	47
Packington's Pound	Anonymous	48

Echos

Stepán Rak

Simple Arpeggios

Reginald Smith Brindle

mf (bring out long notes)

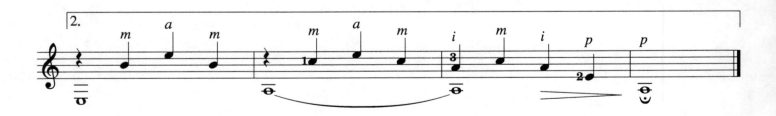

Brindle GUITARCOSMOS 1
© 1979 Schott & Co. Ltd. London
All Rights Reserved
Used by permission of European American Music
Distributors Corporation, sole U.S. and Canadian agent
for Schott & Co. Ltd. London

Aeolian Mode

Reginald Smith Brindle

Brindle GUITARCOSMOS 1
© 1979 Schott & Co. Ltd. London
All Rights Reserved
Used by permission of European American Music
Distributors Corporation, sole U.S. and Canadian agent
for Schott & Co. Ltd. London

Moon Magic

Words by
Christine Kelly

Music by
Sonia Michelson

From *Easy Classic Guitar Solos for Children* by Sonia Michelson. © 1991 by Mel Bay Publications, Inc. All Rights Reserved.

* hold finger down

No. 1 from Three Arpeggio Studies

Reginald Smith Brindle

Brindle GUITARCOSMOS 1
© 1979 Schott & Co. Ltd. London
All Rights Reserved
Used by permission of European American Music
Distributors Corporation, sole U.S. and Canadian agent
for Schott & Co. Ltd. London

Starobylá

Stepán Rak

Rak 26 Humours
© PANTON Ltd. Praha 1985
All Rights Reserved
Used by permission of the Publisher

Country Dance

Reginald Smith Brindle

2nd time rall.

Brindle GUITARCOSMOS 1
© 1979 Schott & Co. Ltd. London
All Rights Reserved
Used by permission of European American Music
Distributors Corporation, sole U.S. and Canadian agent
for Schott & Co. Ltd. London

Allegretto
Op. 44 No. 2

Fernando Sor

Welcome

Gérard Montreuil

from Divertissements, by Gérard Montreuil
© Les éditions DOBERMAN-YPPAN
Used by permission

Allegretto

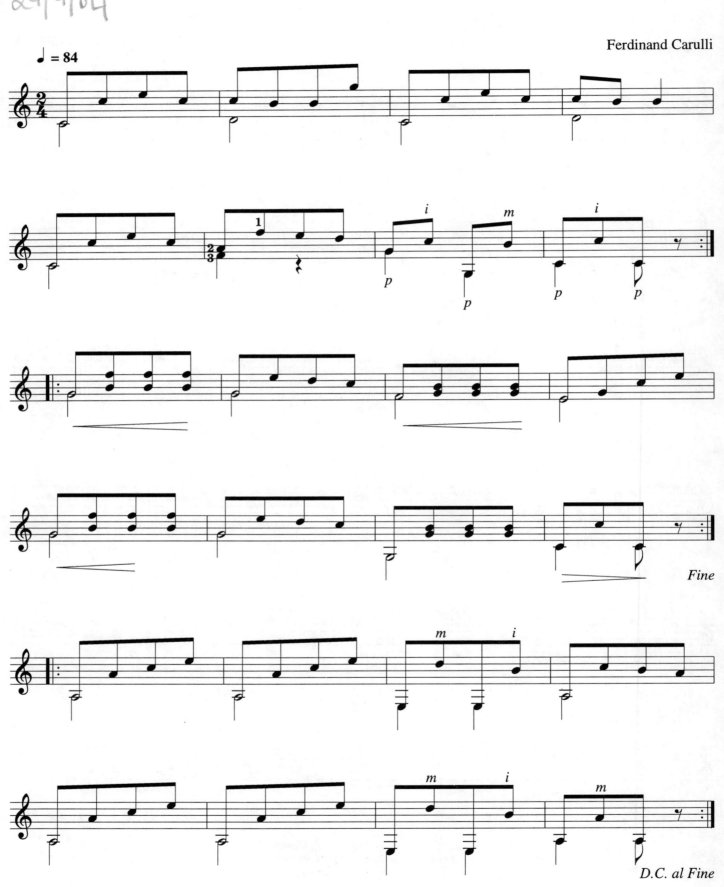

Waltz
Op. 121 No. 1

Danse Russe

From The Magic Guitar
© Les éditions Doberman-Yppan
Used by Permission

Andante

Arr. John Hoffman

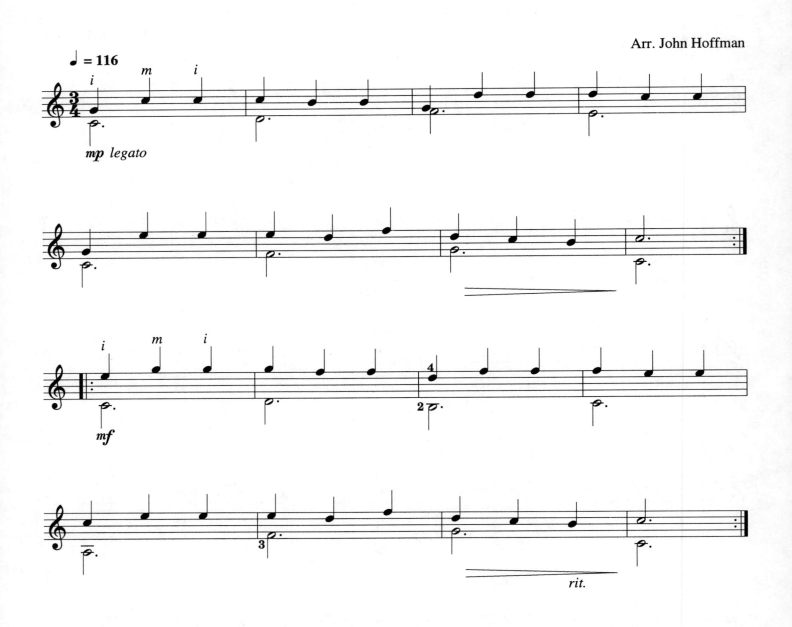

Study In C

Fernando Sor

for Jack Michelson

Sometimes I Hear A Song

Words by
Christine Kelly

Music by
Sonia Michelson

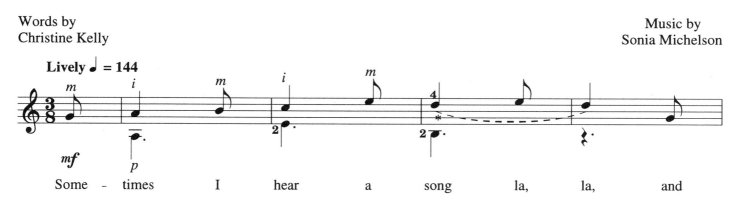

Some - times I hear a song la, la, and

sing it all day long tra, la. I

sing it in the bath tra, la, and

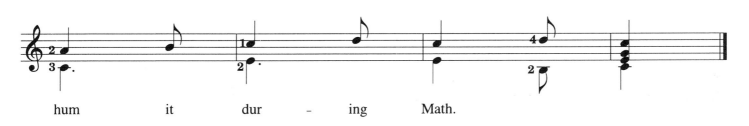

hum it dur - ing Math.

* hold finger down

From *Easy Classic Guitar Solos for Children* by Sonia Michelson. © 1991 by Mel Bay Publications, Inc. All Rights Reserved.

Andante
Op. 31 No. 1

Fernando Sor

Andante
Op. 35 No. 1

Fernando Sor

Allegretto

Fernando Sor

English Dance

Ecossaise
Op. 33 No. 10

Mauro Giuliani

Andantino

Matteo Carcassi

Allegro
Op. 50 No. 13

Mauro Giuliani

Etude

Matteo Carcassi

Prelude
Op. 114

Ferdinand Carulli

Menuett

J. Krieger

Estudio In Am

D. Aguado

Andante

Matteo Carcassi

From *Easy Classic Guitar Solos for Children* by Sonia Michelson. © 1991 by Mel Bay Publications, Inc. All Rights Reserved.

Gigue

J. Logy

Waltz

Ferdinand Carulli

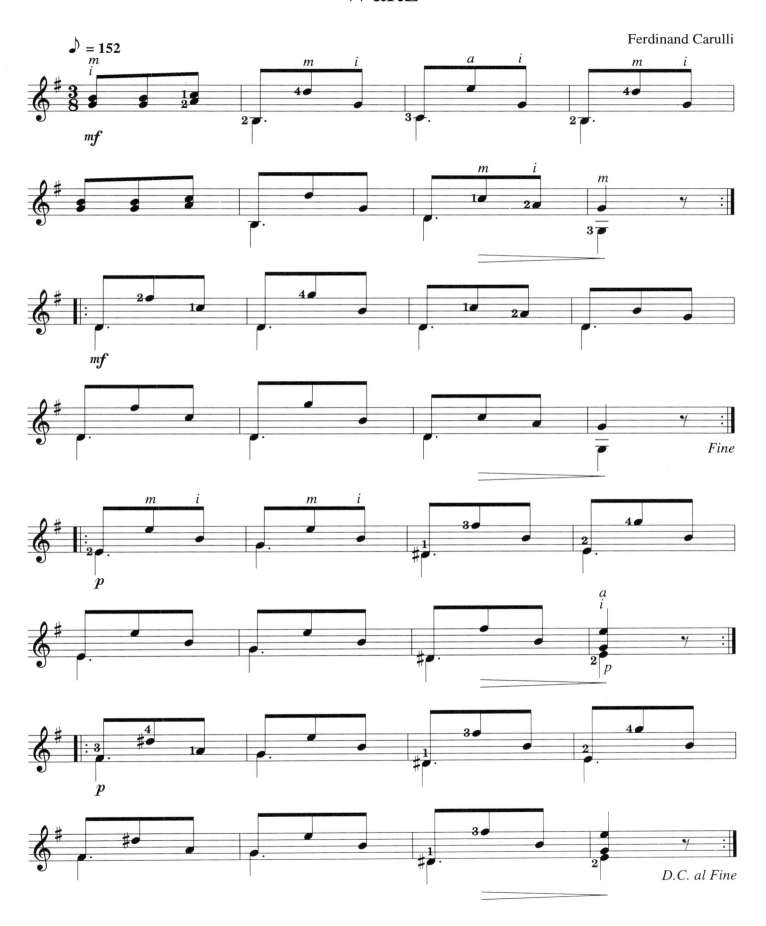

Contre Danse

Vals

Bartolome Calatayud

Minuet

J. S. Bach

Austrian Dance

Arr. John Hoffman

FROM: SONGS AND DANCES FOR GUITAR
© 1966 Theodore Presser Company
Reprinted by permission of the Publisher

for Louis E. Michelson

Prelude In D

Sonia Michelson

*hold finger down

From *Easy Classic Guitar Solos for Children* by Sonia Michelson. © 1991 by Mel Bay Publications, Inc. All Rights Reserved.

German Dance

Arr. John Hoffman

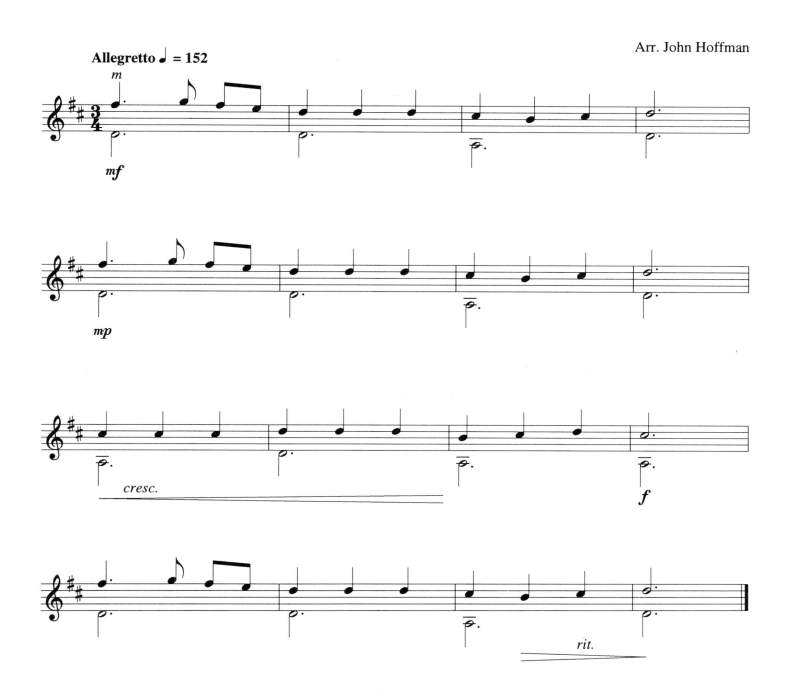

FROM: SONGS AND DANCES FOR GUITAR
© 1966 Theodore Presser Company
Reprinted by permission of the Publisher

Moonlight

English Dance

FROM: SONGS AND DANCES FOR GUITAR
© 1966 Theodore Presser Company
Reprinted by Permission of the Publisher

Spanish Romance

Canario

Carlo Calvi

Packington's Pound

Anon.